Rock 'n' Roll

ROBERT PIOTROWSKI

STECK-VAUGHN
Harcourt Achieve

www.HarcourtAchieve.com

10801 N. Mopac Expressway
Building # 3
Austin, TX 78759
1.800.531.5015

Rubicon © 2006 Rubicon Publishing Inc.
www.rubiconpublishing.com

Project Editors: Miriam Bardswich, Kim Koh
Editor: Amy Land
Creative Director: Jennifer Drew-Tremblay
Art Director: Jen Harvey
Designer: Jan-John Rivera

6 7 8 9 10   5 4 3 2 1

Rock 'n' Roll
ISBN 1-4190-2456-6

CONTENTS

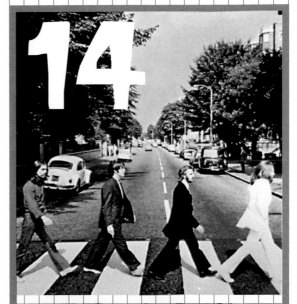

"ROCK 'N' ROLL MUSIC, IF YOU LIKE IT, YOU CAN'T HELP BUT MOVE TO IT. THAT'S WHAT HAPPENS TO ME. I CAN'T HELP IT."
— ELVIS PRESLEY

WHEN ROCK STARTED ROLLING

warm up

With a partner, brainstorm titles of rock 'n' roll songs. What different types of music do you think influenced the musicians who created these tunes?

Although it might feel like rock 'n' roll has been around since the beginning of time, it is only a mid-20th century phenomenon. The term "rock and roll" originated in 1952 when a disc jockey (DJ) named Alan Freed aired a radio show aimed at young music lovers called *Moondog Rock 'n' Roll Party*. But the roots of rock go back even further than that.

phenomenon: *an extraordinary development or occurrence*

Up until the 1950s, many people thought that only African Americans should listen to music created by black artists. This music was labeled "rhythm and blues" (R&B). Much of it had a strong backbeat and harsh singing style. Many people also believed that only whites should listen to music recorded by white artists. This included country and folk, which moved at a slower pace and often told a story.

During this time, African-American artists such as Charlie Christian, Muddy Waters, and B.B. King were making some fantastic music. Meanwhile, white singers like Hank Williams and Bob Wills were making popular songs that mixed a country-music influence with a new style and sound. Music lovers from all backgrounds began to notice. Racial barriers weakened.

CHECKPOINT
What do you think this sentence means?

When these musicians combined their styles, a new type of music emerged. Heavily influenced by R&B traditions, the newly-born rock and roll became very popular among white teens who had already discovered the talents of African-American recording artists. In the early 1950s, airwaves were packed with the music of rock and roll pioneers like Bill Haley, Chuck Berry, Fats Domino, Little Richard, Carl Perkins, and Jerry Lee Lewis. This was music for a younger generation. Rock and roll fit right in with many teenagers' desire to separate themselves from their parents' world. It was fresh and exciting and produced new ways of talking and dressing that most parents didn't understand or approve of. Before long, rock and roll was everywhere.

Unfortunately, even this new brand of music couldn't completely change the racist attitudes of the time. Some record companies recorded white singers performing rhythm and blues songs originally released by black artists. They thought it would make the music seem less threatening. The plan worked — these artists and their covers of R&B songs became very popular.

FYI

The first official rock 'n' roll song to hit #1 was "Rock Around The Clock" recorded by Bill Haley and the Comets in 1955. Haley, a white musician, was influenced by R&B artists.

CHECKPOINT

Why do you think rock 'n' roll music became particularly popular among young people?

Times changed and, eventually, rock 'n' roll did produce numerous performers — both black and white — who enjoyed widespread recognition. The most successful of these was a young man from Memphis, Tennessee. He was a fan of country music but was also very heavily influenced by rhythm and blues performers. His name was Elvis Presley. From the moment he walked on stage and started singing, rock 'n' roll was never the same again.

wrap up

1. What two types of music most strongly influenced rock 'n' roll in the early 1950s?

2. Agree or disagree with the following statement: The history of rock 'n' roll shows that when people from different backgrounds combine their ideas, the result is something good. Use examples from this article and your own research of rock 'n' roll history to support your opinion.

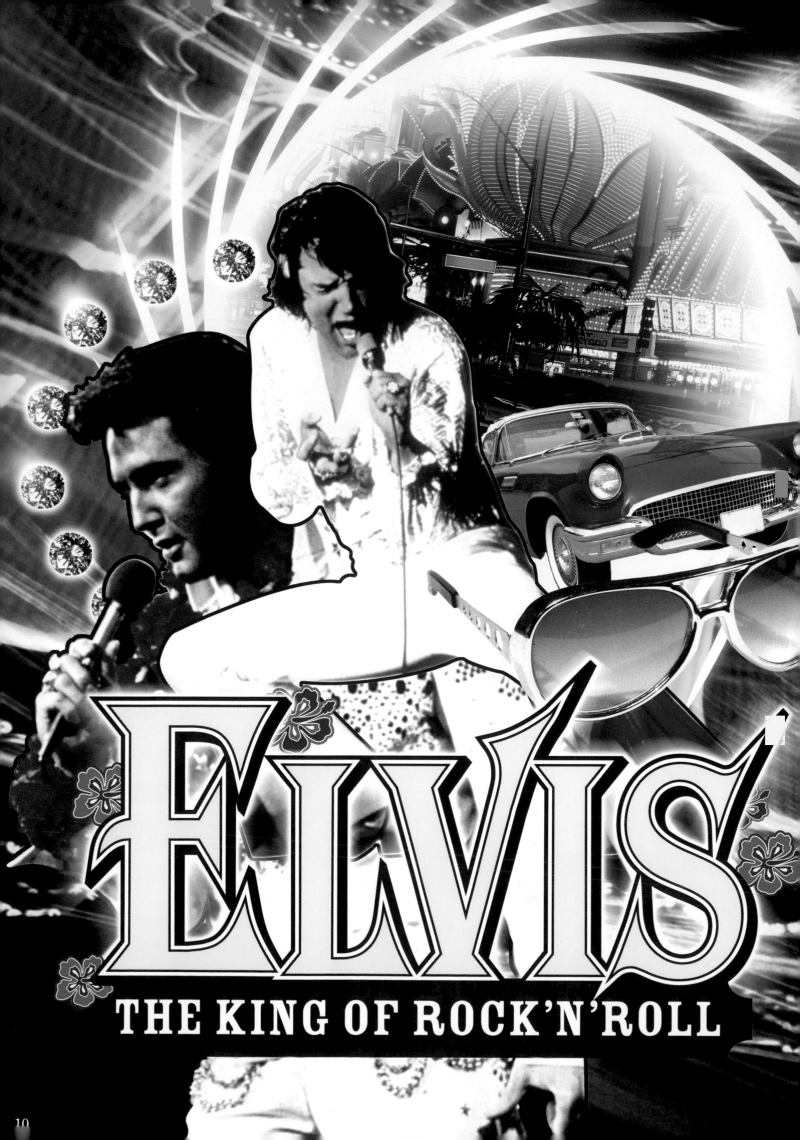

ELVIS
THE KING OF ROCK'N'ROLL

What does it take to become the king of rock 'n' roll? Share your thoughts with a partner.

FULL NAME: Elvis Aaron Presley
NICKNAMES: The King, Elvis the Pelvis, the Hillbilly Cat
BORN: January 8, 1935   **DIED:** August 16, 1977
HOMETOWN: Tupelo, Mississippi; later Memphis, Tennessee

HUMBLE BEGINNINGS: Elvis grew up poor and this made him an outcast in high school. He worked part-time while still a teen to help support his family. After graduation, young Elvis drove a truck for a living and played music at night.

FIRST GUITAR: Elvis's parents bought their preteen son his first guitar. It cost almost $8, which was a lot of money for a struggling family in the 1940s.

BIG BREAK: Elvis recorded a few songs at a local studio to try and impress the owner, Sam Phillips. Elvis's first attempts failed, but the young singer wouldn't give up. Eventually, his rendition of a country song called "That's All Right" made Phillips realize Elvis had talent. The song became so popular that a local radio station played it more than a dozen times in a row.

THE LOOK: Even as a teen, Elvis dyed his hair and combed it like his favorite comic-book heroes and movie stars. His trademark look was completed when he grew long sideburns.

INFLUENCES: Young Elvis was influenced by many different performers. He was a fan of country, gospel, rhythm and blues, and many other musical styles. At the time, Presley was considered unique because he was a white singer whose music sounded like it was being performed by a black artist.

THAT CERTAIN SOMETHING: Elvis had a great voice and movie-star good looks. While on stage, he thrashed his legs and swiveled his hips to the rhythm of the music. Fans loved it. Critics claimed his movements were too sexually suggestive and condemned Elvis's act. As a result, Elvis became the ultimate symbol of rebellion in the 1950s.

NUMBER OF RECORDS SOLD: Over one billion worldwide.

FYI

The King may be dead, but there is no shortage of Elvis impersonators. They come in all shapes and sizes, and they entertain in a variety of ways. The thousands of impersonators are fat, thin, male and female, and of all ages and nationalities. There's everything from the skydiving Flying Elvi to Elvis ministers who perform marriage ceremonies. There is even a Professional Elvis Impersonators Association.

In addition to his singing career, Elvis starred in over 30 hit movies. None of the movies was ever nominated for an Academy Award.

There have been so many reported "Elvis sightings" that the idea that he could still be alive (and hanging out at the 7-Eleven) has become a pop-culture joke.

Elvis's mansion, Graceland, is the second most-visited house in America. The first is the White House.

SPEAKING OF ELVIS...

Check out what these celebs have said about the King.

"Ask anyone. If it hadn't been for Elvis, I don't know where popular music would be. He was the one that started it all off, and he was definitely the start of it for me."

— ELTON JOHN, SINGER/SONGWRITER

"Without Elvis none of us could have made it."

— BUDDY HOLLY, SINGER/SONGWRITER

"That Elvis, man, he is all there is. There ain't no more. Everything starts and ends with him. He wrote the book."

— BRUCE SPRINGSTEEN, SINGER/SONGWRITER

"Before Elvis, there was nothing."

— JOHN LENNON, SINGER/SONGWRITER

"You can't be greater than Elvis, change things as much as the Beatles, or be as original as Led Zeppelin. All you can do is rip them off."

— BILLY CORGAN, SINGER/SONGWRITER

wrap up

Identify the most important information about Elvis in this profile. Using the information, write an obituary and read it to your class or group.

WEB CONNECTIONS

Use the Internet to research your favorite musician. Create a profile for this person using these pages as a guide.

FANTAST

warm up

Some musicians are so famous that they become household names. This means everyone in the country — regardless of his or her taste in music — knows who they are. List all the rock 'n' rollers you can think of who have achieved this level of fame.

In 1964, music history forever changed with five little words: "Ladies and gentleman, the Beatles." This introduction, spoken without much fanfare by Ed Sullivan on his popular TV show, marked the unofficial birth of Beatlemania in North America.

It's hard to argue with the fact that the Beatles are one of the most important and influential bands in rock 'n' roll history — but they didn't start out that way. In fact, the Fab Four began their lives as regular kids from England who happened to have a passion for music.

John Lennon was a troubled boy who was raised by his Aunt Mimi in the mid-1950s. He never saw much of his parents and he wasn't a very good student. Still, young John was a talented artist and a music

IC FOUR

That didn't seem to bother Paul McCartney who thought The Quarrymen sounded great when he caught one of their performances. Paul was also tuned into the arts. Unlike his new friend, John, Paul lived with his mom and dad and got good grades. Before long, Paul joined The Quarrymen, and thus the legendary Lennon/McCartney songwriting team was born.

George Harrison was younger than both John and Paul, but he could really play guitar. George had been encouraged by his mother to learn the songs they listened to on the radio. His outstanding musical talent and the fact that the guys could rehearse at George's house secured his position with the band.

lover. As a teenager he formed a band and named it after the school he attended. The Quarrymen were not a very polished musical act.

"As John, Paul, George, and Ringo continued to write and record, their music changed."

The Quarrymen, renamed the Beatles, were completed with a bass player named Stuart Sutcliffe and a drummer named Pete Best. In 1960, the Beatles played together every chance they got. They moved to Germany for a while to perform in nightclubs. When Sutcliffe quit the band, Paul McCartney took over as bass player. The Beatles performed every night and played into the early morning hours. The guys didn't get paid a lot and nobody knew who they were, but all the hard work began to pay off. They became experienced performers and their impressive musical skills were sharpened during this time.

When they returned to their hometown of Liverpool, England, they began playing at The Cavern Club with other popular bands. At the same time, the guys met two people who would help them on the road to success. One was Brian Epstein. He became their manager and polished up their act. In no time, the Beatles were appearing in the matching suits and mop-top haircuts that made them famous. The second man they met was George Martin.

"Lyrics that were once only about young love matured to cover topics like loneliness and revolution."

He offered the group a record contract. In time George Martin also became their producer and helped the Beatles develop their sound. His influence on the band was so great that he is sometimes called the "fifth Beatle."

C H E C K P O I N T

Why were Brian Epstein and George Martin so important to the success of the Beatles?

But what about Ringo Starr? At the time, he was a popular drummer with another English band named Rory and the Hurricanes. When John, Paul, and George decided to fire Pete Best, Ringo was hired. The Beatles were finally complete.

Their first two records were "Love Me Do" and "Please, Please Me." The music was rhythmic and refreshing. Fans liked the fact that the guys in the band wrote their own songs at a time when most rock 'n' roll musicians did not. John, Paul, George, and Ringo gave hilarious answers to questions interviewers asked them. Young women screamed and fainted during their concerts. England was crazy about the Beatles. Beatlemania had stuck.

In 1964, after the Ed Sullivan appearance, Beatlemania spread to North America. That year, five of Billboard's top 15 songs belonged to the Beatles, including "I Want To Hold Your Hand," which held the number one position. This was the beginning of an era of rock 'n' roll called the British Invasion. During this time performers from Great Britain (whether they were any good or not) found great success in the U.S. and had a huge impact on the American music industry.

The Beatles's popularity continued over the next few years. They released albums, movies, and tons of merchandise. They influenced the way people acted, dressed, and thought about popular music. Teenagers all over the world who heard Beatles's songs were inspired to form their own bands. Everyone had a favorite Beatle and every modern music lover counted down the days until the release of their next record.

CHECKPOINT

Think about how difficult it was for the members of the Beatles to become successful musicians. Why do you think they worked so hard for so long?

As John, Paul, George, and Ringo continued to write and record, their music changed. Lyrics that were once only about young love matured to cover topics like loneliness and revolution. The more the Beatles developed their musical talents, the more people loved them.

A few years later, even though they had been good friends for a while, the Beatles started to drift apart.

A few years later, even though they had been good friends for a while, the Beatles started to drift apart. In 1969, the band broke up. Each member embarked on a successful post-Beatles career. John Lennon wrote and recorded new music with his wife, Yoko Ono. Paul McCartney formed a band called Wings. George Harrison continued to record hit songs and worked in film. And Ringo started the All-Starr Band. Even on their own, the members of the Beatles continued to influence rock 'n' roll.

On December 8, 1980, John Lennon was shot and killed by a fan. The possibility of a Beatles reunion died with him. George Harrison passed away in 2001 from cancer.

The era of the Beatles may be over but their influence on many of today's popular rock 'n' roll performers is undeniable. The songs recorded by these four young men from Liverpool can still be heard blaring from speakers all over the world. Incredibly, more than 40 years after they came together, the Beatles are even more important and more famous than ever.

FYI

Recorded in June 1965, the Beatles's song, "Yesterday," has been recognized by the *Guinness Book of World Records* as the most recorded song in the history of popular music. So far there are over 3,000 different versions by artists like Ray Charles, Boyz II Men, Elvis Presley, and Frank Sinatra.

Paul McCartney is said to have composed "Yesterday" in his sleep. When he woke up, he turned on a tape recorder and quickly played it on his piano so that he wouldn't forget the tune.

A few years after the Beatles broke up, John Lennon made fun of "Yesterday" in a song called "How Do You Sleep?" In the lyrics Lennon tells McCartney, "The only thing you done was yesterday / and since you're gone you're just another day."

wrap up

1. Imagine you are a Beatles fan living in England during the early 1960s. Write a letter to your friend in America who hasn't heard of the Beatles yet. Tell him or her everything you know about this great new band.

2. List all the Beatles's songs you can think of. Compare your list with a partner's.

3. Agree or disagree with the following statement: "The Beatles are the most important band in rock 'n' roll history." Write a paragraph that supports your opinion using facts from the article.

FROM THE KING TO
SIX DECADES OF ROCK 'N' ROLL

1950s ...

- Rhythm and blues and country music hook up and give birth to rock 'n' roll!
- Chuck Berry, Little Richard, Stevie Wonder, Jerry Lee Lewis, and Buddy Holly become the first heroes of rock.
- Elvis is King.

FYI

When rock 'n' roll first appeared in the 1950s, many people thought it was just another passing fad. They didn't expect it to last more than a year or two.

1960s ...

- English bands and singers land in North America during the British Invasion. Their music rockets up the charts.
- The Beatles and the Rolling Stones rule rock 'n' roll.
- Bob Dylan leads the way for a new revolution — folk rock.
- Guitar heroes like Jimi Hendrix electrify the scene while the Beach Boys surf their way to musical success.
- Hippies make a statement at Woodstock, the ultimate music festival.

1970s ...

- Rock bands like Queen and KISS begin to roll.
- Heavy metal steps into the ring against disco; both walk away popular winners, especially Led Zeppelin and the Bee Gees.
- New wave and punk rip away from traditional rock 'n' roll with bands like the Sex Pistols, the Clash, and the Talking Heads.

COLDPLAY

warm up

What important events happened in the past ten years of your life?

1980s ...

- Pop music bops its way into POPularity, led by Michael Jackson and Madonna.
- The launch of MTV makes music videos as important to an artist's success as the music he/she makes.
- The likes of Bon Jovi, Bruce Springsteen, Van Halen, U2, and Guns N' Roses keep rock 'n' roll at the top of the charts.

1990s ...

- Nirvana, Pearl Jam, and Soundgarden bring grunge and alternative music into the spotlight.
- Warning labels appear on albums with potentially offensive lyrics and themes.
- Large-scale festivals like Lollapalooza create a new trend in live music.
- Collaborations and varied influences make it difficult to put bands and performers into specific categories.

2000s + ...

- Rock keeps rollin' in various forms due in part to U2, Weezer, the Killers, Radiohead, Audioslave, Social Distortion, Sheryl Crow, Avril Lavigne, Velvet Revolver, Coldplay, the White Stripes, Foo Fighters, Green Day, the Arcade Fire, Franz Ferdinand, and others.

wrap up

1. Which do you think are the three most important decades in the history of rock 'n' roll? Discuss in a small group.

2. Predict what trends the next ten years will bring in music. Compare your predictions to those of a classmate.

WEB CONNECTIONS

Use the Internet to read about the Rock 'n' Roll Hall of Fame and share the information with your group.

THE GIG

LOWVILLE HIGH

BRRRINGGG!!!

TODAY IS THE LAST DAY OF SCHOOL! IT'S ALSO THE DAY I WILL FINALLY DO SOMETHING I'VE BEEN PLANNING FOR WEEKS ...

... TALK TO THE NEW GIRL.

UM ... HI.

WELL, THAT WAS SORT OF LIKE TALKING

MY UM, MY NAME'S HENRY. HENRY HARRISON. I'M IN YOUR SCIENCE CLASS?

AM I ASKING HER OR TELLING HER THIS INFORMATION?

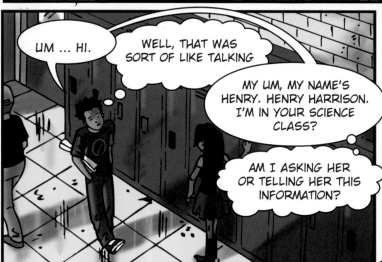

I KNOW. I'M LILLY.

YEAH, HI. ARE YOU GOING TO SUMMERFEST?

DOUBT IT. I'M NOT REALLY INTO CARNIVALS OR WHATEVER.

BUT YOU DON'T WANT TO MISS THIS ONE!

PLAN 9

THE GREATEST PUNK ROCK BAND TO EVER COME OUT OF LOWVILLE APPEARING AT SUMMERFEST 2005 DON'T MISS IT!

SO YOU'RE IN THE GREATEST PUNK ROCK BAND TO EVER COME OUT OF THIS DUMP?

ACTUALLY, THE ONLY. BUT ALSO THE GREATEST.

SO ... WILL YOU? COME TO THE SHOW, I MEAN.

I'LL BE THERE.

Illustrations by DREW NG

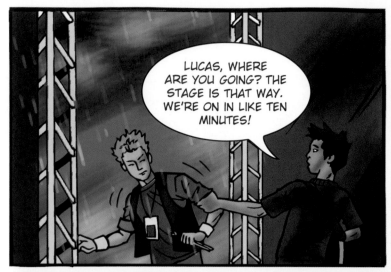

1. How can you tell that Henry is nervous when he is talking to Lilly? What clues in the story reveal Lilly's confident personality? Compare your answers with a partner's.

2. The main character in this story feels more comfortable expressing his feelings through music rather than talking. Find a song whose lyrics symbolize how Henry feels about Lilly. Play the song for your classmates. Give reasons for choosing this particular piece of music.

YOU NAME IT!

How did these great rock 'n' roll bands get their names? Check out the ideas, people, and places that are rumored to have inspired the names of these famous acts ...

warm up

Your name is something you hear every day of your life. If you could choose a new name for yourself, how would you go about deciding on one?

THE ROLLING STONES

These guys named themselves after the title of one of their favorite songs by a famous blues musician named Muddy Waters, whose real name was McKinley Morganfield.

AC/DC

These letters actually stand for "Alternating Current/Direct Current." A sister of one of the band members suggested AC/DC after seeing it on the back of a vacuum cleaner.

FOO FIGHTERS

"Foo fighter" was slang for a UFO back in the days of World War II.

NICKELBACK

A member of this band used to work at a coffee shop. Customers would pay $1.50 for a coffee that cost $1.45 so he spent a lot of time saying, "Here's your nickel back."

WEEZER

weezer

The lead singer of this band had asthma when he was a boy. He was nicknamed "Weezer" because of the noises he made when breathing.

THE BEATLES

Inspired by Buddy Holly and the Crickets, the Fab Four chose to also name themselves after insects. They changed the spelling of *beetles* by replacing the second *e* with an *a* to let their fans know that their songs have a beat.

RAMONES

This group was inspired when Paul McCartney of the Beatles once called himself Paul Ramone to hide his true identity.

IRON MAIDEN

An iron maiden was a torture device used in medieval times. It's a giant coffin lined with sharp spikes. When someone is forced inside and the case is shut, it's a bloody, deadly experience.

BUDDY HOLLY AND THE CRICKETS

The lead singer's name was Buddy Holly. The garage where his band practiced was home to noisy crickets that could be heard in the background during their rehearsals.

CHECKPOINT
What is the connection between Buddy Holly and the Crickets and the Ramones?

Blondie

This name was inspired by something their fair-haired singer heard everywhere she went: "Hey, blondie!"

BLONDIE

GUNS N' ROSES

There once was a band called Hollywood Rose. There once was another band named LA Guns. When members of both bands got together, this name was a no-brainer.

PINK FLOYD

The members of this band were big fans of two other blues musicians named Pink Anderson and Floyd Council.

THE KILLERS

They took their name from an imaginary band in a music video for the song "Crystal" by New Order.

INXS

These four letters were chosen as this band's name because they sound just like the words in excess, which mean "too much."

NIRVANA

NIRVANA

This name ● came from the Buddhist religion. To Buddhists, Nirvana is a place of ultimate peace and freedom.

Red Hot Chili Peppers

They chose their group's name for perhaps the only reason rock 'n' roll bands need to pick a name for themselves — it sounds cool.

BAD NAMES

Call it a hunch, but these not-so-catchy band names probably won't catch on …

Crispy Ambulance
Mr. T Experience
Congratulations on Your Decision to Become a Pilot
Planet of Pants
Big Fat Pet Clams From Outer Space
Dinner is Ruined
Throw That Beat In the Garbagecan
The Elvis Diet
Howard Iceberg and the Titanics
Wookie Chest Hair
Bowling for Soup

wrap up

1. Test your memory. Ask a partner to read the name of a band from the list above. Explain to him or her where the band's name came from without re-reading the article.

2. Create your own unique name for a rock 'n' roll band. Design a cover for a CD case or a poster advertising a concert. Incorporate the band name you made up.

WEB CONNECTIONS

Use the Internet to research the origin of your favorite band's name. Reference at least two sources to ensure you have the correct information.

ROCK 'N' ROLL

In a small group, discuss the popularity of reality TV shows. What is your group's favorite show?

Take some wannabe rockers, some real rockers, a celebrity host ... throw in some classic songs and screaming fans, and what do you get? Well, if the mastermind behind it is reality TV king Mark Burnett (*Survivor* and *The Apprentice*) then you have *Rock Star: INXS* (In Excess). In the summer of 2005, it was the hit show where 15 talented contestants battled it out for the opportunity of a lifetime — a chance at becoming the next lead singer of INXS.

So who is INXS, anyway?

- **This Australian band has had a 25 year career:**
  - **sold 30 million albums**
  - **had No. 1 hits on 4 continents**
  - **played 4,000 live shows to over 25 million people in 50 countries**
  - **coped with lead singer Michael Hutchence's death in 1997.**

◀ Former INXS lead singer
Michael Hutchence (1960-1997)

REALITY

So what happened on the show?

FYI

And the winner was … J.D. Fortune. In the show's final episode, Canadian-born Fortune beat out MiG Ayesa of Australia and Chicago rocker Marty Casey. This 32-year-old former Elvis impersonator showed INXS that he has what it takes to be their new lead singer. Fortune and INXS will record an album and go on a world tour in early 2006.

- **15 contestants** competed in **39 episodes**
- **viewed for 13 weeks** by over **5 million fans**
- **1 winner was chosen.**

wrap up

Create a poster to announce INXS's world tour in 2006. Use the information from these pages.

WEB CONNECTIONS

There were several personalities involved in *Rock Star: INXS.* Use the Internet to research someone from the show (it could be the creator, a band member, or contestant). Using the information you've found, write a profile of this person.

MY CONFESSION

warm up

Have you ever been in a situation when you were misunderstood by your family or friends? How did you try to make these people understand your actions? Were you able to convince them?

"My dad and I used to get along really good, then he told me to get out."

Dear Everybody,

First of all let me say I'm not sorry. I know you all think I busted that window for no reason. But you're wrong. Let me tell you what it really was.

My name is Marco Montonacci. I'm 18. I live in the basement apartment of my Aunt Lucille's house. My dad and I used to get along really good, then he told me to get out. Actually, what he said was that I couldn't play my music under his roof anymore. So I took off. And up until a few hours ago, I was glad I did.

Music is everything to me. I'm the drummer in a band called Klut-Z. Kind of a cross between The Red Hot Chili Peppers and Green Day. I think we've got a good chance of making it. Right now we're working on this demo. It's smokin'. But my father was never into it.

We didn't talk at all after I moved out to Aunt Lucille's. I think he always felt I should try to be more than a musician. Maybe a businessman. Or a landscaper like him. Truth is, I always wanted to play guitar. But I'm built like my dad. Pop's hands are strong and small. So are mine. Too small to stretch over enough frets to make me the next Jimi Hendrix. I took up drums instead. They sound good and I can hit them all I want. Let my anger out. It's helped build up my arms. I think they look good. I cut the sleeves off every T-shirt I own.

"It made me feel like a kid. Being in that place, waiting to see my father after his heart attack, wanting to hide something that is part of me. I hate feeling like that."

That's what I was wearing earlier today at the hospital, baggy jeans and a cut-off Iron Maiden tee. It looks alright on stage and on the street, but in the hospital everyone had suits and ties, or at least sweaters.

The tattoo on my wrist was showing and I didn't have any way to cover it up. It's my name written in Chinese characters. The hospital receptionist stared at it when I came in.

It made me feel like a kid. Being in that place, waiting to see my father after his heart attack, wanting to hide something that is part of me. I hate feeling like that. It makes me want to punch something. But I don't do that anymore. Instead, I escape into my music. It never fails me.

CHECKPOINT
What do you do to escape from the world when you feel stressed?

Even when I was really young, I remembered this little tape deck Pop had bought me. I carried it everywhere. One time I even took it on a job with him. I think it was a day off from school or something. He woke me up early and we were in his truck before the sun was all the way out. Then we were on some rich man's lawn digging and sweating together. The radio was cranked. Even though he knew I loved music, my dad made me shut it off after an hour. Then he told me to listen.

"You hear that, Marco?" he asked.

I didn't. The only thing going on was some birds chirping and somebody's lawn mower going a few backyards away.

"That's my music." He repeated it in Italian and pointed to his chest. "*Mia musica*."

I didn't get it. For the rest of the afternoon I interrupted his instructions to me repeatedly, begging to have the radio back on. Finally he allowed it.

That had been a long time ago. I was trying to figure out how long exactly when Lucille appeared in the hospital hallway. My Aunt is a beautiful woman. But she did not look it today. I'm not sure why but when I saw her, I stood up right away and started walking. I had to turn back, of course, and let my aunt lead me. I had no idea where Pop's room was.

She told me he had been cutting some patio stones in his driveway. He always liked everything perfect. At noon a neighbor had spotted him lying face down on the asphalt.

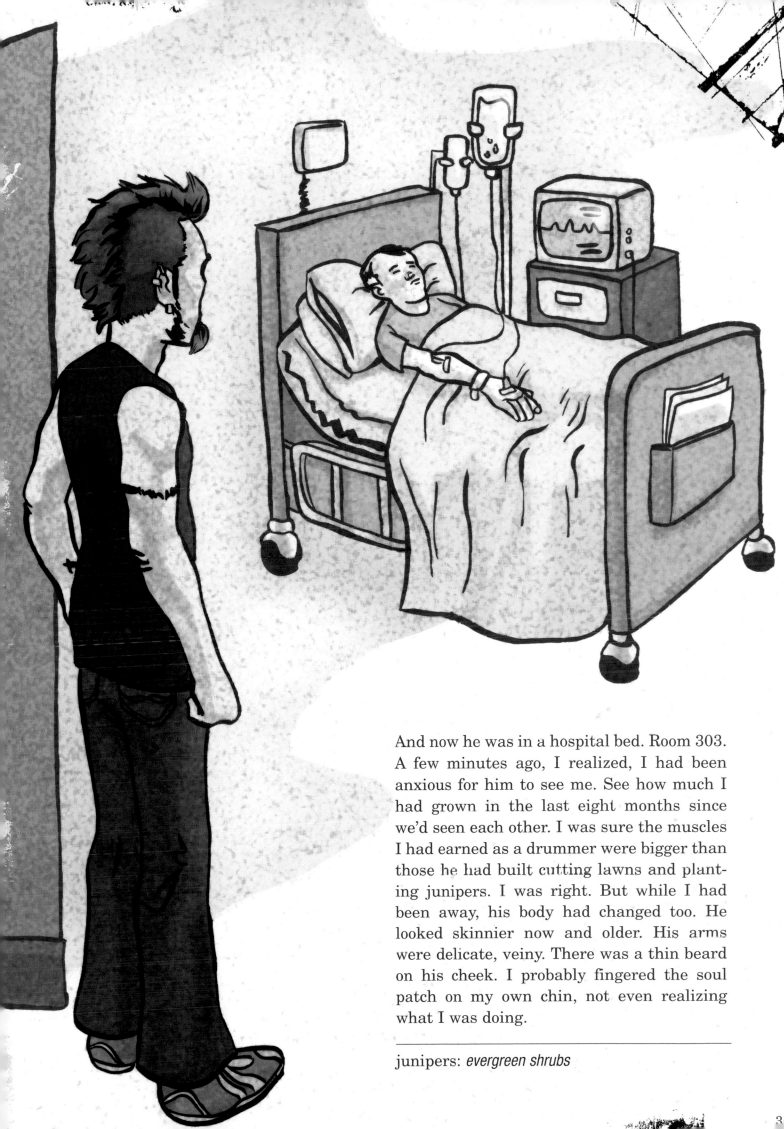

And now he was in a hospital bed. Room 303. A few minutes ago, I realized, I had been anxious for him to see me. See how much I had grown in the last eight months since we'd seen each other. I was sure the muscles I had earned as a drummer were bigger than those he had built cutting lawns and planting junipers. I was right. But while I had been away, his body had changed too. He looked skinnier now and older. His arms were delicate, veiny. There was a thin beard on his cheek. I probably fingered the soul patch on my own chin, not even realizing what I was doing.

junipers: *evergreen shrubs*

When I left his house last winter, my father was a proud man. Now he was a puddle of bones with tubes eating into his skin. I sat down slowly beside him.

"It's me, Pop. Marco."

He didn't answer. Aunt Lucille put her hand on my shoulder. I just sat and watched my father's stillness.

A plastic glint caught my eye. It was my father's hospital ID bracelet. I fingered it and read the personal information printed there. So now both of us had our names on our wrists. Mine was there forever. I'd rip his off in a second if I could. Then I'd smash up the whole room like a rock star.

CHECKPOINT
Notice how Marco expresses his feelings in this paragraph.

"*Proprio adesso non è in grado di parlare,*" Lucille said from over my shoulder. "*Ma so che è lieto che sei qui.*" I had to translate the words from Italian into English inside my head. He can't talk right now. But I know he is happy that you are here.

"I don't know. Maybe not," I told her without turning around. I couldn't take my eyes off him. He was so small.

"Don't talk like that, Marco. He is your father. He loves you very much."

"I know." I admitted it quietly.

"He gave up everything for your mother and you. Came to America against his family's wishes. Started his business from nothing. All for you and your mamma."

It's true. My father defied my grandfather and the rest of his family. He left Italy — left everything — to run his own business and make a living doing something he loved. That was big-time rebellion in those days. And although I had known all this ever since I can remember, it suddenly sounded familiar for the first time.

---

glint: *flash*

defied: *resisted*

"I'm sorry you didn't understand me, Pop."

It sounded like me.

I wanted to tell him I had figured it out. I wanted so badly for Pop to wake up then.

"I'm sorry," I would have said. "I'm sorry you didn't understand me, Pop. And that I didn't recognize how important your work was. Being outside and making gardens look their best meant everything to you. Even if I do make it as a musician, I'm sorry."

I would have told him. But he couldn't wake up. And it was too late.

CHECKPOINT
How has Marco's attitude toward his father changed?

The machines attached to my father started going crazy then. A number of nurses rushed in trying to save him. There was no room near the bed anymore so my aunt and I stood and watched by the window.

My father was dying. I wanted to do something for him. Something, I guess, that I hope someone would do for me if I were dying inside a hospital room. I thought about running out and getting some music. But that was ridiculous.

Next thing I knew, my fist went through the window and three people were holding my arms and yelling. My knuckles were bleeding.

I know you think I'm just a punk kid who punched out a window because I was angry. Maybe I would have done that a couple of years ago. But not anymore. Or you're saying it's because I want attention or hate my father or something. But I don't. I love him. I'm just like him. That's why we didn't get along.

The reason for what I did is very simple.

The windows in that room aren't the kind that open. And I wanted my father to hear his music — the song of the outdoors — one more time before he was gone.

So I'm not sorry. I would do it again. How can I be so sure it was the right thing? Because it's what I would have wanted too. *Mia musica*. Pop's music may have been different from mine, but it was everything to him. Just like mine is to me. I understand that now. My only regret is not having figured it out sooner.

wrap up

1. In your own words, explain why Marco broke the window in the hospital room.

2. Rewrite the ending of this story with Marco's father recovering from his heart attack. What do you think Marco's father would say to him if he had the chance to speak to his son again?

THIS SCHOOLHOUSE ROCKS!

By Jim Trzaska

warm up

After reading the title, discuss with a partner what you think this article will be about.

Sure, the Ramones sang about it in the 80s, but until recently, the idea of a rock 'n' roll high school existed only on the radio airwaves. Imagine music lessons that are more Beatles than Beethoven, where students not only practice their instruments but also learn performance skills, and where recitals are actually full-scale concerts with light shows and smoke machines. Welcome to Philadelphia's Paul Green School of Rock Music!

Since the spring of 2000, when founder Paul Green moved the lessons he was giving out of his apartment into an actual building, the School of Rock has been teaching kids ages 12 to 17 the art of rock 'n' roll. With approximately 150 students and 10 instructors, the school offers classes in vocals, guitar, bass guitar, drums, keyboards, and more. Recent concerts included tributes to classic rock legends like Pink Floyd and Led Zeppelin, and students have performed for local audiences, as well as in venues in New York City and Texas.

THIS AIN'T *AMERICAN IDOL* ...

According to bass instructor Dylan McConnell, who has been teaching at the School of Rock for three years, auditions for school admission are rare. "Anyone who is interested and dedicated enough is welcome," he says. In fact, many students enroll after they see their friends perform in shows, even if they have no prior musical experience.

CHECKPOINT
Why do you think students with no experience suddenly want to enroll?

And instead of focusing on pop-rock artists like blink-182 and No Doubt, students mostly learn and perform the music of classic rock artists like Queen and Frank Zappa. Despite the fact that these musicians had their heyday before many of the students were even born, the school's budding musicians still

heyday: *peak of their success*

"They come here with the desire to hear something real and substantial, and to learn where today's music came from."

appreciate their creativity and technique. "I've never come in contact with a student who wasn't into it because it's 'old stuff,'" claims Dylan. "They come here with the desire to hear something real and substantial, and to learn where today's music came from."

Sixteen-year-old Eric Slick, who used to listen mainly to bands like Nirvana, Foo Fighters, and Bush, now cites the eclectic music of Frank Zappa as his favorite to perform. "It tends to bring out the best in every musician," he says. "It's the most challenging, fun to play, and definitely gets the best crowd reaction."

I'M WITH THE BAND

Since playing in his first showcase — a tribute to Pink Floyd's *The Wall* album almost five years ago — Eric has gone on to perform in front of a crowd of almost 6,000 at Texas' Wild Flower Music Festival. He's also looking forward to traveling to Germany later this year with 23 other students to play at the 14th Annual Zappanale Festival. Back home, he teaches at the school, and works on its official website.

Dylan is confident that students who want a career in music will leave the School of Rock with the skills and experience they need to make it in the music industry. In fact, he and some other instructors have been known to make picks of which students we'll be seeing on the cover of *Rolling Stone* in 10 years. One former student is already playing with a band that toured in the Vans Warped Tour this summer.

Given its high standard of skill and professionalism, it's only a matter of time before the School of Rock starts producing other success stories that will end up one day on MTV and at the top of the charts. And to that, we say, "Rock on!"

eclectic: *coming from various sources*

CHECKPOINT
How would performing in front of 6,000 people make you feel?

"It's only a matter of time before the School of Rock starts producing other success stories that end up one day on MTV."

wrap up

Write an email to a friend telling him/her all about the School of Rock. Be sure to include why you would or wouldn't want to go to this school.

PRIDE

warm up

Rites of passage are things that people do, say, or receive to symbolize that they have entered new eras in their lives. A rite might be formal like a graduation ceremony, or informal like getting your first part-time job or your driver's license. List three rites of passage that you have experienced in your life.

In 1984 I was awkward and shy. That was just me back then. My older sister, Karen, was the exact opposite. She had gone away to college in September and returned home for the holidays more stunning than ever. I hated her a little bit for that. But I still loved her. She was my sister, after all.

I didn't have a date that Saturday night. As a matter of fact, I had only ever been out on two real dates. Each had shown up at my door in a tie, carrying a single red rose. I kept those flowers pressed inside the pages of my favorite issue of *Seventeen* magazine as keepsakes. Karen — with her wild smile and dark eyes — lived in a world where Saturday nights meant choices between the track star with dance tickets and the economics major with the Mercedes. Truth is, I thought my sister's dating habits were rather shallow. That didn't change the fact that I envied her.

Earlier that evening I had helped Karen squeeze into a pair of jeans so tight she'd had to lie flat on my bed to zip them up. Seven hours later I found myself tracking those same jeans across the dark hallway leading from my room. It was 2 AM. I had been sleeping soundly when Karen woke me. At first I thought something was terribly wrong. A fire. A burglar. Maybe World War III. But Karen silently assured me that there was no need for alarm, only stealth.

"The trailer. Come on." My sister motioned for me to follow her.

As we tiptoed toward the stairs, Karen suddenly stopped in front of our parents' bedroom door. I didn't notice and kept walking straight into her! We smacked together like something out of a Three Stooges movie.

"Shhh…" Karen made the noise as much for her own benefit as mine.

---

stunning: *beautiful*

stealth: *secrecy and quiet*

We froze, expecting our parents to stir behind their closed door. I didn't know what Karen had planned, but my insides — still powdered with the memory of slumber — began to twinge with excitement. Standing there in secret passage with my sister, I felt anything was possible.

CHECKPOINT
What type of relationship does the writer have with her sister?

Karen had been out with one of her boyfriends, Chad, earlier that night. So maybe he had a younger brother whom Karen had brought home for me. I imagined Chad's brother waiting to meet me in our crammed trailer — artsy and painfully

slumber: *sleep*
artsy: *a person who enjoys the arts: music, visual art, literature, etc.*

handsome like Sting or the lead singer from Duran Duran.

Once Karen and I were sure that my mom and dad had not heard us, we crept downstairs and headed for the front door. I stopped in the hall to slip bare feet into a pair of runners. Karen waited patiently before leading me outside.

The night air broke what was left of my drowsiness. The street, though, was still asleep.

"Come on." We sprang down our porch steps and across the front lawn.

My dad had bought the old camping trailer years ago. This box-on-wheels was parked in our driveway; it had stood there ever since I could remember. In grade school, Karen and her friends had used it as a secret clubhouse. Now, years later, she was finally inviting me inside. But why?

My sister entered the trailer and held the spring-loaded door for me. It took my eyes a few moments to adjust to the dim light inside. The trailer smelled like a suitcase. I looked around wildly, searching for the reason my sister had dragged me out here, hoping that it was worth the trouble we could get into for sneaking out of the house at this hour.

The only thing waiting for me was a tape deck.

CHECKPOINT
Predict what surprise Karen has for her sister.

Karen motioned for me to sit on a low bench that stretched across one of the trailer's walls. She planted herself on the floor in front of the stereo. Wordlessly, she pressed the eject button and the gray thing spat out a cassette. My sister extracted it with manicured thumb and forefinger, flipped it, and inserted the tape back into the deck. In the second or two that she held the cassette, I read two characters on a piece of masking tape stretched across it.

U2

Their meaning was the furthest thing from my mind. I wanted Chad's brother, even if he didn't exist.

"This is the second song on the album," Karen announced. She pressed Play without any further explanation. Was this some kind of college-girl prank?

characters: *letters and numbers*

What more, in the name of love...

Suddenly a lazy electric guitar and a tattoo of drums cut through the inside of the trailer. Karen cranked the volume. Under normal circumstances I would have been worried about waking my parents —

One man come in the name of love . . .

But by then the singer had begun to belt out words and I was lost in them.

One man come and go . . .

We sat in silence, listening to the song, letting the music and lyrics wash over us.

In the name of love,
What more, in the name of love . . .

"Where did you get that tape? Who are these guys?" I asked when the song ended.

"Chad gave it to me. They're called U2. They're from Ireland. I think this is their fourth album or something but they're totally underground. Aren't they amazing?"

"U2." I let the name sit in my mouth before allowing it to escape through my lips.

"This song is called 'Pride.' Wanna hear it again?"

tattoo: *a steady rhythm*
underground: *outside the mainstream*

I did. We stayed in the trailer for the next hour just listening to the rest of that U2 album. It was funny. I had never even heard of this band before that night but somehow all the songs including "Pride" sounded familiar. Like all U2 had done was take the music I had inside me and released it to play out loud. I think Karen felt the same way.

When the tape finished, we talked. Karen told me about how fun it was in college, being on her own and doing whatever she wanted. The only problem was Chad wasn't there. In the middle of the night, while we sat there becoming friends my sister confessed her love for him. I was the first to know.

I told Karen I was happy for her. But that wasn't enough. I felt I needed to share something too. Something deep and personal. Something I would have kept to myself before the trailer and the U2 tape. So I confessed about wishing she had set me up with Chad's brother. I wanted it to sound exotic and personal. Instead, the secret revealed itself as absurd — especially after Karen told me that Chad's only brother was three years old. We laughed about that until our throats ached. It felt good to get the laughter out and leave my childish hopes of romance behind.

CHECKPOINT

How has the writer's relationship with Karen evolved since the beginning of the story? What brought on this change?

exotic: *unusual, foreign*
absurd: *silly, crazy*

"But after those couple of hours in the trailer, I had somehow become more like myself."

When it was time to go back to the house, I wanted to take Karen's U2 tape with us. I wanted to tell my sister to at least hide it in case somebody broke into the trailer that night and stole it. But I didn't. Instead, I just walked back into the house, this time with Karen trailing behind me, and went up to my room.

I didn't stop to see if my parents were up or not. I suppose I didn't care if they caught me sneaking back in. What could they do to me?

I wasn't sure exactly what had changed. Earlier, I had wanted a date with my sister's boyfriend's non-existent brother more than anything. I had wanted to be more like Karen. But after those couple of hours in the trailer, I had somehow become more like myself.

Pride. What a perfect title for a piece of music.

It sounds silly, I know. Being that affected by a song and a conversation with someone you have known your whole life! But I guess that's just the way I was in 1984. And I'm happy to say not much has changed since.

wrap up

1. In a short paragraph, describe the relationship between the two sisters before and after the night in the trailer.

2. What would you say to the singer/band of your favorite song if you could talk to them? Script a dialogue between yourself and this person or group telling them how much their work means to you. Practice with a partner and present your script to the class.

ACKNOWLEDGMENTS

The publisher gratefully acknowledges the following for permission to reprint copyrighted material in this book.

Every reasonable effort has been made to trace the owners of copyrighted material and to make due acknowledgment. Any errors or omissions drawn to our attention will be gladly rectified in future editions.

Jim Trzaska: "This Schoolhouse Rocks!" is reprinted with permission from teenwire.com. For more articles, please visit teenwire.com.